W9-BRA-592

'29

429

796.426
NENT

Nentl, Jerolyn.

Marathon running.

DATE DUE	BORROWER'S NAME	ROOM NO.
SEP 1 4 1982	Kevin 7	
MAR 2 3 1983		
acct 4/19/84	Donald W.	6

429

796.426
NENT

Nentl, Jerolyn.

Marathon running.

306200 09905C

MARATHON RUNNING

MARATHON RUNNING

by Jerolyn Ann Nentl

Library of Congress Catalog Card Number: 79-27799

International Standard Book Number:
    0-89686-074-4 Library Bound
    0-89686-078-7 Paperback

Designed & Produced by Randal M. Heise

Edited by - Dr. Howard Schroeder
            Prof. in Reading and Language Arts
            Dept. of Elementary Education
            Mankato State University

Library of Congress
Cataloging in Publication Data

Nentl, Jerolyn Ann.
  Marathon running.

  (Funseekers)
  SUMMARY: Discusses the history of marathon running,
the marathon races now existing, famous runners, running
records, and possible injuries that improper care may in-
cure.
  1. Marathon running--Juvenile literature. (1. Marathon
running. 2. Running) I. Schroeder, Howard. II. Title. III.
Series.
GV1065.N45   796.4'26   79-27799
ISBN 0-89686-074-4

Photo Credits

Globe Photos: 3
Janeart, Ltd: 5, 8, 11, 14, 15, 16, 17, 19, 20, 21, 23, 24, 27A, 27B, 28,
    29, 30, 31, 32
Dave Drennen: 6, 25
Bosten Globe: 12A
Bettmann Archive: 12B
United Press International: 13
Nike: 23B

Joe caught sight of his car and slowed himself down to a gentle jog. He had been running hard for more than an hour, but was not out of breath. As a matter of fact, he had never felt so good! Running in the early hours of the morning made his whole day seem better.

Slipping into his warm-up clothes, Joe let himself dream a little. For the last few mornings, he had been thinking about running in a marathon. The run today had been about ten miles. The route had been mostly flat, with a few small hills. He had made it over them with ease. He wondered how far he could run. A marathon would be about twenty-six miles. He felt he could do it.

The thought of being in a marathon excited Joe. He knew it was a special group. If Joe trained all summer, he might be ready for a fall marathon. Maybe Joan would like to try running one, too. She jogged with a few friends every afternoon after work. On weekends, she had been running some longer distances in the country.

Joe made up his mind to talk to her about it that evening. Perhaps the coaches at the high school could tell them how to train.

A marathon is not a simple "fun run." It is a long, often painful test of a runner's strength and ability to last the distance. Many long-distance races are called marathons. The real marathon is a race exactly 26.218 miles long.

Marathons are not all alike since the courses over which the races are run are different. Some are flat while others are hilly. One course winds to the top of a mountain in Colorado called Pike's Peak and back down again. Some are in the country while others go through town. The New York City Marathon goes through twelve neighborhoods and across five bridges. This makes it difficult to compare marathon times. What is fast for one course may be slow for another. Times over the same courses may also change because of the weather. Wind and temperature can affect the speed a marathoner can run.

Courses may stretch from point-to-point. They may go in laps around a circle. They may loop out to a point and back again. No matter how a course is laid out, it must be measured exactly. Marathon races can be open or restricted. Open races welcome any runner. Beginners may find themselves in the same race as a world champion! Restricted races limit who may run. This is done in different ways:

- age
- sex
- experience
- qualifying times

The marathon, as we know it today began in 1896. That was the year the Olympic Games were revived in Greece. A twenty-four-mile foot race was part of the games in honor of a Greek named Pheidippides. In 490 B.C., he ran twenty-four miles from the Plains of Marathon to Athens to announce the Greek victory over the Persians. Then he died. The story may not be true, but it does not matter. It reflects the mood of the modern marathon race — endurance under stress. Today, the Olympic Marathon is one of the most well-known races in the world.

Pheidippides, the first marathon runner.

Frank Shorter, winner of the 1972 Olympic Marathon race.

Paavo Nurmi (far right) is known as the father of long distance running.

The marathon course was increased to its odd length in 1908. The games were held in London that year. Since the royal family wanted to watch, the Olympic officials changed the route so it would go by their box seat. This stretched the course to 26 miles and 385 yards or 26.218 miles. That length was made the standard Olympic marathon distance in 1924.

A Greek runner won the first Olympic marathon with a time of 2:58:50. That means 2 hours, 58 minutes and 50 seconds. The United States won the race in 1904 and again in 1908. They did not win again for sixty-four years. Then, in 1972, Frank Shorter won the race in Montreal, Canada, with a time of 2:12:20. He had run his first marathon only a year before.

The fastest man in history is Derek Clayton of Australia. He ran a marathon race in 2:08:34 in 1969. This record still stands.

Paavo Nurmi, from Finland, is called the father of long-distance running. He never entered an Olympic Marathon, but was a runner for twenty years. His only goal was to better his own time. Nurmi's style is said to be the best. He used an easy stride, with the heel touching the ground first. His body and head were held erect.

Marathon runners bring in the Olympic flame at the start of the 1972 Olympic Games in Munich, Germany.

Another early long-distance runner was Emil Zatopek of Czechoslovakia. He won the 1952 Olympic race in 2:23:04 without ever before having run a marathon! Zatopek was as clumsy as Nurmi was graceful, and made awful faces as he ran. He would roll his head and wave his arms. It looked as if he were in great pain.

Abebe Bikila of Ethiopia won the 1960 Olympic race running barefooted! He took off his shoes at the start of the race because they were giving him blisters. His time was 2:15:17. Bikila won again in 1964 in 2:12:12. This time he wore shoes. In 1969 he was in a car accident and was paralyzed from the waist down. This ended his career as a runner. Bikila is the only man to have won two Olympic marathons.

The famous marathon runners so far have all been men. Women were not allowed to enter the long-distance races until the last few years. The first woman marathoner in the United States was Roberta Gibb. In 1966, she hid in the bushes at the Boston Marathon. When the gun went off, she slipped in among the male runners. She crossed the finish line with a time of 3:21:02. The next year, Kathy Switzer became the first woman to run at Boston wearing a race number. She had registered as K. Switzer. When it was discovered that K. Switzer was a woman, the men tried to put her out of the race. A male friend came to her aid and she kept on running. Kathy finished in 4:20:02. Women could not legally race in the Boston Marathon until 1972. They still may not run in the Olympic Marathon. Instead, women hold their own world-wide race.

Veteran marathon runner, John Kelly, keeps up the pace at the '79 Boston Marathon.

Running for fun and health had become popular in the United States in the 1960's. The marathon became a goal for many of these runners. Frank Shorter's 1972 Olympic win had made running look fun!

Today, marathons are run by thousands of men, women and children. Brent Bogle ran one at the age of four in 6:03:35. Jennifer Amyx ran 4:00:36 when she was six years old. Mavis Lindgren was clocked at 4:42:49 when she was seventy-one years old. Paul Spangler ran a marathon in 3:59:47 when he was seventy-nine years old.

Almost anyone who is healthy can run a marathon. To run one without injury, a person must train. Training gets a runner's body and mind in shape. No runner should try a marathon race until he or she can run ten to fifteen miles often without having problems. The serious marathoner may run fifty miles a week during training. Top marathoners may run more than one hundred miles a week!

Loosen up!

All training is based on stress. It is called "getting in shape." If the body is "pushed" to its limits, and then just a little bit more, it grows stronger. If it is pushed too much, there is an injury. Progress must come slowly if a runner is to stay healthy. Runners and coaches have learned that the body's heart and lungs get into shape quicker than the feet and legs.

Running long distances at low speed builds endurance. Sprinting, or running a short distance as fast as a person can, helps build speed. A runner's endurance can be greatly improved by training. Speed can be increased only a small amount. How fast a runner can go often depends on body structure at birth.

Marathon runners must train each day of the year, no matter what the weather. Finding time to train is a problem for many runners. Some like to train early in the morning. Others do it at lunch time. Still others prefer the end of the work day or the cool of the evening. Some even train at night.

Most runners keep a training diary. They list when and how far they run. They describe each workout and the shape they are in at the time. Some runners list the weather, their weight and the type of shoes they wore.

Whether training or racing, runners must watch for any sign that they are overstressing their bodies. This is the best way to avoid injuries. A runner's feet and legs ache when they are tired. So does a runner's heart and

lungs. If runners ignore the warning signs, they may injure themselves. Training time will be lost while they get better, and they may miss some races. They may have to give up running if they seriously hurt themselves.

Warm-up exercises help prevent injuries, too. They stretch and loosen tight muscles. A runner eases into each stretched position, holding it for a few seconds. Bouncing, jerky movements do not help.

Proper rest and food are needed, too. Rest gives the body time to heal itself so it can run again. Bad eating habits may cause a loss of strength. Sometimes runners get headaches if they do not eat well. Their eyesight may blurr, too.

All runners must guard against heat stroke. It can cause death unless a runner's body temperature is lowered quickly. It is for this reason runners must drink plenty of water. They must drink even if they are not thirsty. Some marathoners pour water over their bodies to help keep themselves cool.

Proper exercises must be done before the running starts. A runner must stretch and loosen those tight muscles.

Improper running may cause other injuries, too:

- Blisters and bruises.
- Stress fractures. These are small cracks in the bone which can be found only with X-rays. They can be quite painful, but often heal much faster than broken bones.
- Sore muscles.
- Shin splints. This is a dull ache in the muscles in the front of the leg.
- Side stitch. This is a severe side-pain.
- Lower back pain.
- Blackened toenails. This is caused by shoes that do not have enough room for the runner's toes.
- Knee problems.

A runner's whole body is jarred when his feet pound the ground. Good shoes help cushion this stress. There are two types of running shoes made — training shoes and racing flats. Training shoes are sturdy and have extra support. Racing flats are lightweight with thinner soles. They help a runner go fast during a race.

There are hundreds of styles in running shoes being made today. No matter which a runner chooses, the shoes must fit properly. Running shoes must be kept in good repair, too. Rough edges inside a shoe can cause blisters during a long run. Worn soles can cause ankle or knee problems.

Protect your feet with proper running shoes.

Training shoes   *Racing flats*

23

When the day of a race arrives, a runner is anxious to meet the challenge. Many marathoners take a pre-race jog of one or two miles. It helps calm their nerves and loosen their muscles. Once the gun goes off, planning is important. Marathoners running their first race often start out too fast. It is better to hold back, saving the runner's energy for later in the race.

"The wall" is the nickname given to that point in the marathon when a runner is out of energy. Some runners can force themselves beyond the wall. If they are near the finish line, they might make it. If they are not, they will have to drop out of the race. This is why smart marathoners start out slowly. They choose a pace they can hold throughout the race. Runners going the same speed sometimes talk to each other to help pace themselves.

Going uphill sometimes pushes the marathon runner to "the wall."

Women do not hit the wall as often as men. This may be because they know how to pace themselves better. They may also have a larger store of energy, since they are not built as lean as male runners.

Most runners have aches and pains in their muscles toward the end of a marathon. Some put all their attention on the pain they are feeling to help push themselves to the end. Others can make it only if they ignore the pain and think of something else.

Once across the finish line, marathoners do not just stop running. They coast to a jog and then a walk, or run in place for awhile. This gives their bodies a chance to cool down. Meanwhile, computers turn out the race results. A runner's best time is called his or her "personal record," or PR. Each race offers a chance to better one's PR.

After a marathon race, runners must allow their bodies time to recover. For some runners, this takes only five to ten days. For others, it may be three weeks or longer. Runners do not stop training during this time, but they do not stress themselves at all.

Running a marathon is a challenge. It is not something a runner does every day. Experts used to think a person could not run more than two good marathons a year. Now people are running four without hurting their bodies.

There are about 350 marathons a year. Most of them are held in the United States. Marathoners race in all the fifty states, even Alaska. They race in Canada, Japan, and Europe, too. The four largest marathons in the U.S. are held in New York City, Honolulu, Boston, and Chicago.

The New York City Marathon is the largest foot race in the world. Ten thousand runners entered it in 1978. One thousand of them were women. The Boston Marathon is the oldest long-distance race in the United States. It was first held in 1897, one year after the first Olympic Marathon. No Olympic Marathon winner has won at Boston, although eight have tried. The race is popular with non-runners, too. At times those watching the race outnumber the runners 100 to 1!

The Chicago Race is called the Mayor Daley Marathon. It is at the end of a fitness week held in that city each year. In 1978, there were more than five thousand runners.

Bill Rogers, winner of the 1975, '78 and '79 Boston Marathon, crosses the finish line (above). Below, Rogers wears the Victory Wreath and gives the victory signal after the 1979 race. His time was 2:09:27.

To replace lost body fluids, runner's grab a drink "on the run."

Hawaii has a long tradition of running, too. The Honolulu Marathon is a race of celebration! Long ago, the King's Runners carried the news around the islands. Today, these people run for fun. There are more runners in Hawaii than anywhere else in the United States.

One of the best marathons is held in Japan. Any Japanese who has run a marathon in 2:20 or better may enter. Only invited foreign runners may compete. Those who are fifteen minutes behind the leader at the halfway point are out of the race. After the halfway point runners who lag thirty minutes behind are out.

Tough as they may be, these races are not enough for some runners. They want to test their skills even more. For these runners, there are "ultramarathons." These are longer races than the standard marathon. There has been a 72-mile ultramarathon around Lake Tahoe. A 145-mile race has been run across Death Valley. A race from coast to coast is being planned, too. There are also races to see how far someone can run in a set amount of time, such as a 24-hour marathon. These races demand mental toughness as

All the hard work is forgotten when you cross the finish line in first place.

well as endurance. Much can go wrong during such a long race. There is a great chance of injury and illness. For this reason, ultramarathoners are older, more experienced runners.

Runners enter marathons for many reasons. The old tradition of the race appeals to some runners. Most just want to find out if they can meet the challenge and succeed. Can they run that far? Can they handle the mental stress of pushing their body to its limit?

For most marathoners, the reward is not trophies or laurel wreaths. The reward is this new knowledge about themselves. It is a reward most non-runners find hard to understand. Runners say it makes the many days of training and pain worth it.

The men's marathon record is 2:08:34 set by Derek Clayton in 1969. The women's record is being broken often. In 1979 it was 2:27:33. This was set by Grete Waitz of Norway. How fast will men and women be able to run the race? Only the future will tell.

Back Bay Trail ←

OFFICIAL
BOSTON
MARATHON
SPECTATOR